The Fifth Line

Limericks After Lear

Book One

John Arthur Nichol
Illustrations by Rory Walker

Text Copyright © John Arthur Nichol 2020

Illustrations Copyright © Rory Walker 2020

All Rights Reserved

Edward Lear's verses are in the public domain.

ISBN
978-0-6489059-0-5 (paperback)
978-0-6489059-1-2 (ePub)
978-0-6489059-2-9 (mobi)

 A catalogue record for this work is available from the National Library of Australia

Cover Illustration Copyright © Rory Walker 2020

For Jeff, Dave and Pete. Always.

Contents

Foreword 12

The Limericks 15

A Man With a Nose 16

A Person of Smyrna 17

A Man on a Hill 18

A Person of Chili 19

A Man With a Gong 20

A Man of Kilkenny 21

A Man of Columbia 22

A Man in a Tree 23

A Lady of Chertsey 24

A Lady Whose Chin 26

A Man With a Flute 27

A Lady of Portugal 28

A Person of Ischia 29

A Man of Vienna 30

A Man in a Boat 31

A Person of Buda 32

A Man of Moldavia 33

A Person of Hurst 34

A Man of Madras 35

A Person of Dover 36

A Person of Leeds 37

A Person of Cadiz 39

A Man of the Isles 40

A Person of Basing 41

A Man Who Supposed 42

A Person Whose Habits 43

A Man of the West 44

A Man of Marseilles 46

A Man of the Wrekin 47

A Lady Whose Nose 48

A Lady of Norway 49

A Man of Apulia 50

A Man of Quebec...51

A Lady of Bute...52

A Person of Philoe..54

A Man With a Poker..55

A Person of Prague..56

A Man of Peru..57

A Man of the North..58

A Person of Troy...59

A Person of Mold...60

A Person of Tring..61

A Man of Nepal..63

A Man of the Nile...64

Man of th' Abruzzi..65

A Man of Calcutta..66

A Person of Rhodes...67

A Man of the South...68

A Man of Melrose..69

A Man of the Dee...70

A Lady of Lucca 71

A Man of Coblenz 72

A Man of Bohemia 73

A Man of Corfu 74

A Man of Vesuvius 75

A Man of Dundee 77

A Lady Whose Folly 78

A Man On Some Rocks 79

A Person of Rheims 80

A Man of Leghorn 81

A Man In a Pew 82

A Man of Jamaica 83

A Man Who Said How 84

A Lady of Troy 85

A Lady of Hull 86

A Person of Dutton 88

A Man Who Said Hush 89

A Lady of Russia 90

A Lady of Tyre 91

A Person of Bangor 92

A Man of the East 93

A Man of the Coast 94

A Man of Kamschatka 95

A Person of Gretna 96

A Man With a Beard 97

A Man of Berlin 98

A Man of the West 99

A Person of Cheadle 100

A Person of Anerley 101

A Lady of Wales 102

A Lady of Welling 103

A Person of Tartary 104

A Man of Whitehaven 105

A Lady of Sweden 106

A Person of Chester 107

A Man of the Cape 108

A Person of Burton 110

A Person of Ems 111

A Girl of Majorca 112

A Lady of Poole 113

A Lady of Prague 114

A Lady of Parma 115

A Person of Sparta 116

A Man On Whose Nose 117

A Lady of Turkey 118

A Man of Aosta 119

A Person of Crete 120

A Lady of Clare 122

A Lady of Dorking 123

A Man of Cape Horn 124

A Person of Cromer 125

A Man of the Hague 126

A Person of Spain 127

A Man Who Said Well 128

A Man With an Owl 129

A Man in a Casement 130

A Person of Ewell 131

A Man of Peru 132

A Man With a Beard 133

A Lady Whose Eyes 135

A Lady of Ryde 136

A Lady Whose Bonnet 137

The Next Hundred Lears 138

Sascha Martin's Rocket-Ship 139

Thank You 141

Illustrations

A Travelling Lass of the Firth 25

An Old Person of Leeds 38

An Old Man of the West 45

A Young Lady of Bute 53
A Young Lady of Tring 62
An Old Man of Vesuvius 76
A Young Lady of Hull 87
An Old Man of the Cape 109
A Young Person of Crete 121
A Man Who Was Cheered 134

Foreword

Edward Lear didn't invent the limerick. But when he published *A Book of Nonsense* in 1846, he inspired many other writers to adopt the form, and the limerick has been a part of popular culture in every generation since.

Limericks have a defined form that is immediately familiar: five lines in a pattern of two long, two short, one long, with a rhyme shared by the long lines, and another rhyme shared by the short lines.

Limericks in this form existed well before Lear, and Lear cited, as the model for his own efforts, the following verse quoted to him by a friend:

There was an old man of Tobago,
Lived long on rice-gruel and sago
Till, much to his bliss,
His physician said this -
'To a leg, sir, of mutton you may go.'

This is a proper limerick, in every sense.

But Lear himself did not as a rule write proper limericks.

Lear threw away the most powerful feature of the form: the fifth line, where a limerick concludes with a twist and is rendered satisfactory.

Edward Lear discarded the fifth line in function, and he rejected it symbolically as well, by combining lines three and four, the short lines, into a single third line. The disabled fifth line then became the fourth, and Lear used it merely to repeat the essence of what he'd said in the first line (or occasionally the second).

There was an Old Person of Ischia,
Whose conduct grew friskier and friskier;
He danced hornpipes and jigs, and ate thousands of figs,
That lively Old Person of Ischia

In *The Fifth Line: Limericks After Lear*, I mean after in the sense of inspired by or based upon.

Each of Lear's verses from *A Book of Nonsense*, I've used as the starting point for a new limerick that reinstates the fifth line and restores its purpose.

For some verses I've developed several alternatives, in which case I've tried to select (and it's often been a compromise) the version I think is the funniest, the best formed, and the one most suited to a general audience.

Some of Lear's verses are difficult to adapt using his leading rhymes. Lear didn't need three rhyming words for his long lines; he only needed two, since his last line would repeat the final word of the first. So while Lear could happily begin with ...

There was an Old Lady of Chertsey ...

it is all but impossible to turn that beginning into a proper limerick. There aren't enough rhyming words. In cases like this, I've had to turn things around.

In some of my limericks I've remained close to Lear's original premise, as established in his first two lines. In others I've taken a different direction ... sometimes wildly different; but that's a limerick's particular delight, that it takes the writer where it wants to go.

A difficulty I faced with some of Lear's rhymes was his Englishness. Edward Lear, for instance, rhymed *hush* with *bush*, and *Hull* with *bull*, but outside England those rhymes don't work at all. At times I have adopted Lear's vowel sound, even though I would pronounce a word differently. Where this may cause confusion, I have marked the relevant words in bold italic, like ***this***.

Lear sometimes bends the sound of a place name to suit his purposes, as when he rhymes *Prague* with *vague* or *plague*. This practice falls within the finest tradition of limericks, for a lady who rides on a tiger may indeed hail from Riga (or Niger). I've followed Lear's lead in some cases, and diverged in others.

Above all, I've tried to make my limericks fun. I hope you enjoy them.

John Arthur Nichol, Sydney, 2020

The Limericks

Each page after this will show first
A poem that Mr Lear versed;
Then its recent extension
By me, an invention
In limerick format immersed.

A Man With a Nose

There was an Old Man with a nose,
Who said, "If you choose to suppose
That my nose is too long, you are certainly wrong!"
That remarkable Man with a nose.

  Edward Lear

There was a Young Man with a nose,
With two eyes, and with brows over those,
And a mouth and a chin;
But before we begin ...
He had all of his fingers and toes.

A Person of Smyrna

There was a Young Person of Smyrna,
Whose Grandmother threatened to burn her;
But she seized on the Cat, and said, "Granny, burn that!
You incongruous Old Woman of Smyrna!"

Edward Lear

There was a Young Person of Smyrna,
Whose Grandmother threatened to burn her;
She was ever so good
But they'd run out of wood,
And she'd never been much of an earner.

A Man on a Hill

There was an Old Man on a hill,
Who seldom, if ever, stood still;
He ran up and down in his Grandmother's
gown,
Which adorned that Old Man on a hill.

Edward Lear

There was an Old Man on a hill
Who seldom, if ever, stood still;
He ran up to the crown
In his Grandmother's gown,
So he wouldn't come down with a chill.

A Person of Chili

There was an Old Person of Chili,
Whose conduct was painful and silly;
He sate on the stairs, eating apples and pears,
That imprudent Old Person of Chili.

Edward Lear

There was an Old Person of Chile
Who bought a Peruvian Lily,
Which he showed, to impress,
In its national dress,
And a pot that was puffy and frilly.

A Man With a Gong

There was an Old Man with a gong,
Who bumped at it all the day long;
But they called out, "Oh, law! you're a horrid old bore!"
So they smashed that Old Man with a gong.

   Edward Lear

There was an Old Man with a gong,
Who bumped at it all the day long;
For his friends, Pianola,
And Flute and Viola,
Had told him he didn't belong.

A Man of Kilkenny

There was an Old Man of Kilkenny,
Who never had more than a penny;
He spent all that money in onions and honey,
That wayward Old Man of Kilkenny.

Edward Lear

There was an Old Man of Kilkenny
Who wandered the fields on a jenny;
He was quick on the count
When he had to dismount,
Cause he never spent more than a penny.

A Man of Columbia

There was an Old Man of Columbia,
Who was thirsty, and called out for some beer;
But they brought it quite hot, in a small copper pot,
Which disgusted that man of Columbia.

   Edward Lear

As the waiter was chewing his head,
The old man gave a laugh, and he said,
"Oh, the zombies are zombier
Back in Colombia!
Stop it and bring me some bread!"

A Man in a Tree

There was an Old Man in a tree,
Who was horribly bored by a Bee;
When they said, "Does it buzz?" he replied,
"Yes, it does!
It's a regular brute of a Bee."

Edward Lear

A highwayman held up a bee;
"Give me all of your honey!" said he.
But the bee, lacking honey,
Said "Please! I have money!
My wallet's up there in the tree!"

A Lady of Chertsey

*There was an Old Lady of Chertsey,
Who made a remarkable curtsey;
She twirled round and round, till she sank underground,
Which distressed all the people of Chertsey.*

Edward Lear

*A Travelling Lass of the Firth
Spun around till she entered the earth;
And emerging in Chertsey,
She offered a curtsey,
And said, "I was aiming for Perth."*

A Travelling Lass of the Firth

A Lady Whose Chin

There was a Young Lady whose chin
Resembled the point of a pin;
So she had it made sharp, and purchased a
harp,
And played several tunes with her chin.

Edward Lear

There was a Young Lady whose chin
Much resembled the point of a pin;
It was sharp as her tongue,
And it cut as she swung,
So her visitors wouldn't come in.

A Man With a Flute

There was an Old Man with a flute,—
A "sarpint" ran into his boot!
But he played day and night, till the "sarpint"
took flight,
And avoided that Man with a flute.

Edward Lear

There was an Old Man with a flute,
And cobra-skin footwear, to boot;
So his shoes, when he'd play,
Would arise with a sway
And run off, with the man in pursuit.

A Lady of Portugal

There was a Young Lady of Portugal,
Whose ideas were excessively nautical;
She climbed up a tree to examine the sea,
But declared she would never leave Portugal.

Edward Lear

A Portuguese Mariner's Daughter
Cherished all that her father had taught her;
And she longed to be free,
With the wind and the sea,
But alas, she was scared of the water.

A Person of Ischia

There was an Old Person of Ischia,
Whose conduct grew friskier and friskier;
He danced hornpipes and jigs, and ate
thousands of figs,
That lively Old Person of Ischia.

Edward Lear

There was an Old Dancer of Ischia,
Whose movements of old had been friskier;
He could still do a number
On anyone's rumba,
But disco he found to be riskier.

A Man of Vienna

There was an Old Man of Vienna,
Who lived upon Tincture of Senna;
When that did not agree, he took Camomile
Tea,
That nasty Old Man of Vienna.

Edward Lear

There was an Old Man of Vienna
Who wrote his life story in henna
On the walls of the loo
While transitioning through
The effects of a Tincture of Senna.

A Man in a Boat

There was an Old Man in a boat,
Who said, "I'm afloat! I'm afloat!"
When they said, "No, you ain't!" he was ready
to faint,
That unhappy Old Man in a boat.

Edward Lear

There was an old man with a goat,
Who said, "I'm afloat! I'm afloat!"
Though the goat was alarmed
It continued, unharmed,
Eating grass by the side of the boat.

A Person of Buda

There was an Old Person of Buda,
Whose conduct grew ruder and ruder,
Till at last with a hammer they silenced his clamour.
By smashing that Person of Buda.

Edward Lear

There was an Old Person of Buda,
Who couldn't have been any cruder;
So they thought he was best
Relocated to Pest,
Where the people were generally ruder.

A Man of Moldavia

There was an Old Man of Moldavia,
Who had the most curious behaviour;
For while he was able, he slept on a table,
That funny Old Man of Moldavia.

Edward Lear

There was an Old Man of Moldavia,
Who moved to the heart of Belgravia;
He'd been known over there
By his name, Xavier,
But the Londoners thought he was Xavier.

A Person of Hurst

There was an Old Person of Hurst,
Who drank when he was not athirst;
When they said, "You'll grow fatter!" he
answered "What matter?"
That globular Person of Hurst.

  Edward Lear

There was an Old Person of Hurst
Who drank from a bucket and burst;
So he died with a wave
That was tidal and grave,
And the village below was immersed.

A Man of Madras

There was an Old Man of Madras,
Who rode on a cream-coloured Ass;
But the length of its ears so promoted his fears,
That it killed that Old Man of Madras.

Edward Lear

A Lass Lacking Luck in Madras
Slipped and fell in a mucky morass;
She emerged in a gown
That was muddy and brown,
To be shunned by her cream-coloured Ass.

A Person of Dover

There was an Old Person of Dover,
Who rushed through a field of blue clover;
But some very large Bees stung his nose and
his knees,
So he very soon went back to Dover.

Edward Lear

There was an Old Person of Dover,
A person of standing, moreover,
So to say, in a way,
For he stood every day
At the cliff, till a wind blew him over.

A Person of Leeds

There was an Old Person of Leeds,
Whose head was infested with beads;
She sat on a stool and ate gooseberry-fool,
Which agreed with that Person of Leeds.

Edward Lear

There was an Old Person of Leeds
Whose bed was infested with swedes;
So he sat on a stool,
Feeding gooseberry fool
To a turnip invested with needs.

An Old Person of Leeds

A Person of Cadiz

There was an Old Person of Cadiz,
Who was always polite to all ladies;
But in handing his daughter, he fell into the water,
Which drowned that Old Person of Cadiz.

Edward Lear

A Confident Man of Cadiz
Had the waviest hair that there is;
But in contact with water,
The hair of his daughter
Would turn to a bundle of frizz.

A Man of the Isles

There was an Old Man of the Isles,
Whose face was pervaded with smiles;
He sang "High dum diddle," and played on the fiddle,
That amiable Man of the Isles.

  Edward Lear

There was an Old Man of the Isles,
Whose animals wandered for miles;
He'd ensured they were taught
In the quadruped sport
Of surmounting unmountable stiles.

A Person of Basing

There was an Old Person of Basing,
Whose presence of mind was amazing;
He purchased a steed, which he rode at full
speed,
And escaped from the people of Basing.

Edward Lear

There was an Old Person of Basing,
Who walked, for the movement was bracing;
But he'd stop, with a frown,
At the edge of the town ...
To continue would just be debasing.

A Man Who Supposed

*There was an Old Man who supposed
That the street door was partially closed;
But some very large Rats ate his coats and his hats,
While that futile Old Gentleman dozed.*

Edward Lear

*An Old Man had fallen asleep,
But the door was still open a peep;
He awoke to the dawn
With a powerful yawn,
And a bed full of slumbering sheep.*

A Person Whose Habits

There was an Old Person whose habits
Induced him to feed upon Rabbits;
When he'd eaten eighteen, he turned perfectly green,
Upon which he relinquished those habits.

Edward Lear

There was an Old Person whose Rabbits
Had adopted the fellow's own habits;
They would dress in a cowl,
With a book and a scowl,
And debate in the Council of Abbots.

A Man of the West

There was an Old Man of the West,
Who wore a pale plum-coloured vest;
When they said, "Does it fit?" he replied, "Not a bit!"
That uneasy Old Man of the West.

Edward Lear

There was an Old Man of the West
Who woke with a seal on his chest;
Though he dealt it a blow,
It refused to let go,
And he couldn't fit into his vest.

An Old Man of the West

A Man of Marseilles

There was an Old Man of Marseilles,
Whose daughters wore bottle-green veils:
They caught several Fish, which they put in a dish,
And sent to their Pa at Marseilles.

Edward Lear

There was an Old Man of Marseilles,
Whose daughters were elfin and fey;
But their airy, ethereal
Dressing material
Frightened the fishes away.

A Man of the Wrekin

There was an Old Man of the Wrekin,
Whose shoes made a horrible creaking;
But they said, "Tell us whether your shoes are
of leather,
Or of what, you Old Man of the Wrekin?"

Edward Lear

There was an Old Man of the Wrekin,
Who would dress in a manner Mohican;
He was fearsomely quaint
In his feathers and paint,
But they still let him serve as a deacon.

A Lady Whose Nose

There was a Young Lady whose nose
Was so long that it reached to her toes;
So she hired an Old Lady, whose conduct was steady,
To carry that wonderful nose.

Edward Lear

There was a Young Lady whose nose
Was so long that it reached to her toes;
But it looked as it ought,
For her body was short,
Which is where the confusion arose.

A Lady of Norway

There was a Young Lady of Norway,
Who casually sat in a doorway;
When the door squeezed her flat, she
exclaimed, "What of that?"
This courageous Young Lady of Norway.

Edward Lear

There was a Young Lady of Norway,
Who casually sat in a doorway;
She was dreamily braiding,
And thinking of raiding,
Instead of surviving the poor way.

A Man of Apulia

There was an Old Man of Apulia,
Whose conduct was very peculiar;
He fed twenty sons upon nothing but buns,
That whimsical Man of Apulia.

Edward Lear

There was an Old Man of Apulia,
Whose conduct was quaint and peculiar;
For, whomever he'd meet
And engage on the street,
He would always address them as Julia.

A Man of Quebec

There was an Old Man of Quebec,—
A beetle ran over his neck;
But he cried, "With a needle I'll slay you, O beadle!"
That angry Old Man of Quebec.

Edward Lear

A Seafaring Man of Quebec,
Turned his galleon into a wreck,
By releasing the wheel
With a womanly squeal
When a beetle ran over his neck.

A Lady of Bute

There was a Young Lady of Bute,
Who played on a silver-gilt flute;
She played several jigs to her Uncle's white
Pigs:
That amusing Young Lady of Bute.

   Edward Lear

There was a Young Lady of Bute
Who climbed an enormous green shoot;
It led up to a cloud
That was leaky and loud,
So she bought an umbrella en route.

A Young Lady of Bute

A Person of Philoe

There was an Old Person of Philoe,
Whose conduct was scroobious and wily;
He rushed up a Palm when the weather was calm,
And observed all the ruins of Philoe.

Edward Lear

A soldier of fortune in Philoe
Found a scorpion right on his li-lo;
In his sudden alarm
He ascended a palm,
While the scorpion finished his Milo.

A Man With a Poker

There was an Old Man with a poker,
Who painted his face with red ochre.
When they said, "You 're a Guy!" he made no reply,
But knocked them all down with his poker.

Edward Lear

Said the Frog Matching Service, Avoca,
"If the frog is as fair as you spoke her,
And you want to be seen,
Then you cannot stay green!
You must cover your face in red ochre."

A Person of Prague

There was an Old Person of Prague,
Who was suddenly seized with the plague;
But they gave him some butter, which caused him to mutter,
And cured that Old Person of Prague.

Edward Lear

A wealthy old Person of Prague
Was abed with a terrible ague;
For his personal nurse
It could all have been worse,
Because everyone else had the Plague.

A Man of Peru

There was an Old Man of Peru,
Who watched his wife making a stew;
But once, by mistake, in a stove she did bake
That unfortunate Man of Peru.

Edward Lear

There was an Old Man of Peru,
Who fell in a simmering stew;
And his vision grew dimmer
The more he would simmer,
But gee he was easy to chew.

A Man of the North

There was an Old Man of the North,
Who fell into a basin of broth;
But a laudable cook fished him out with a hook,
Which saved that Old Man of the North.

   Edward Lear

There was an Old Man of the North,
Who opened his door and went forth;
But if only he'd stirred
Then he could have gone third,
So he vowed to leave sooner, henceforth.

A Person of Troy

There was an Old Person of Troy,
Whose drink was warm brandy and soy,
Which he took with a spoon, by the light of the moon,
In sight of the city of Troy.

Edward Lear

"I want soy!" Helen pouted, upset.
What she wanted she wasn't to get;
For the homeland of soy
Was in Asia, not Troy,
And they hadn't discovered it yet.

A Person of Mold

There was an Old Person of Mold,
Who shrank from sensations of cold;
So he purchased some muffs, some furs, and some fluffs,
And wrapped himself well from the cold.

Edward Lear

There was a Young Lady of Mold
Who slumped on a tuffet and lolled;
Along came a spider
That loudly decried her,
And told her at once to unfold.

A Person of Tring

There was an Old Person of Tring,
Who embellished his nose with a ring;
He gazed at the moon every evening in June,
That ecstatic Old Person of Tring.

Edward Lear

There was a Young Lady of Tring,
Who'd leap in the air and take wing;
For her mum was a fairy,
But Father was wary,
And tethered them both on a string.

A Young Lady of Tring

A Man of Nepal

There was an Old Man of Nepaul,
From his horse had a terrible fall;
But, though split quite in two, with some very strong glue
They mended that man of Nepaul.

Edward Lear

There was a Young Lass of Nepal
Who covered her head with a shawl,
And went slack on the back
Of her powerful yak,
For the traffic had slowed to a crawl.

A Man of the Nile

There was an Old Man of the Nile,
Who sharpened his nails with a file,
Till he cut off his thumbs, and said calmly,
"This comes
Of sharpening one's nails with a file!"

Edward Lear

There was an Old Man of the Nile,
Who thought happiness utterly vile;
He was never so glad
As when sorry and sad,
And would faint at the hint of a smile.

Man of th' Abruzzi

There was an Old Man of th' Abruzzi,
So blind that he couldn't his foot see;
When they said, "That's your toe," he replied,
"Is it so?"
That doubtful Old Man of th' Abruzzi.

Edward Lear

There was an Old Man of th' Abruzzi,
Who'd constantly trip on his footsie;
In his anger and rage
He examined a page
That examined the stance of the Tutsi.

A Man of Calcutta

There was an Old Man of Calcutta,
Who perpetually ate bread and butter;
Till a great bit of muffin, on which he was stuffing,
Choked that horrid Old Man of Calcutta.

Edward Lear

There was an Old Man of Calcutta,
Who liked to play golf in the gutter;
But his balls were a pain
When they fell in the drain,
Cause he couldn't quite reach with his putter.

A Person of Rhodes

There was an Old Person of Rhodes,
Who strongly objected to toads;
He paid several cousins to catch them by dozens,
That futile Old Person of Rhodes.

Edward Lear

There was an Old Ruler of Rhodes,
Whose letters were written in codes;
And he sent them abroad
By amphibian horde,
Knowing none could decipher his toads.

A Man of the South

*There was an Old Man of the South,
Who had an immoderate mouth;
But in swallowing a dish that was quite full of
Fish,
He was choked, that Old Man of the South.*

Edward Lear

*There was a Young Man of the South,
Who would swear when he opened his mouth;
But in keeping it closed
He was fit, he supposed,
To converse with the Ladies of Louth.*

A Man of Melrose

There was an Old Man of Melrose,
Who walked on the tips of his toes;
But they said, "It ain't pleasant to see you at
present,
You stupid Old Man of Melrose."

Edward Lear

There was an Old Man of Melrose,
Whose talk was all yesses and nos;
He would never expand
On the matter at hand,
And if pressed, he would stand on his toes.

A Man of the Dee

There was an Old Man of the Dee,
Who was sadly annoyed by a Flea;
When he said, "I will scratch it!" they gave
him a hatchet,
Which grieved that Old Man of the Dee.

Edward Lear

There was an Old Man of the Dee,
Who epically fought with a Flea;
At the height of the battle,
The terrified cattle
Were driven to chamomile tea.

A Lady of Lucca

There was a Young Lady of Lucca,
Whose lovers completely forsook her;
She ran up a tree, and said "Fiddle-de-dee!"
Which embarrassed the people of Lucca.

Edward Lear

There was a Young Lady of Lucca,
And someone's chihuahua mistook her
For a post or a tree,
So it ventured a wee,
And her every companion forsook her.

A Man of Coblenz

There was an Old Man of Coblenz,
The length of whose legs was immense;
He went with one prance from Turkey to
France,
That surprising Old Man of Coblenz.

Edward Lear

A man of great stride, in Coblenz,
With a step would have been in Bregenz;
Due to Covid afflictions,
The travel restrictions
Confined him to bed, in a sense.

A Man of Bohemia

There was an Old Man of Bohemia,
Whose daughter was christened Euphemia;
But one day, to his grief, she married a thief,
Which grieved that Old Man of Bohemia.

Edward Lear

There was an Old Man of Bohemia,
Who christened his daughter Euphemia;
And his coffee, when right,
Was a little bit white,
But Euphemia made it much creamier.

A Man of Corfu

There was an Old Man of Corfu,
Who never knew what he should do;
So he rushed up and down, till the sun made him brown,
That bewildered Old Man of Corfu.

Edward Lear

There was an Old Man of Corfu,
Who was fond of a sausage or two;
When his daughter, named Megan,
Would visit (a Vegan),
He had to make do with tofu.

A Man of Vesuvius

There was an Old Man of Vesuvius,
Who studied the works of Vitruvius;
When the flames burnt his book, to drinking he took,
That morbid Old Man of Vesuvius.

Edward Lear

There was an Old Man of Vesuvius,
Who'd studied the works of Vitruvius;
And the home he built under
The mountain, a wonder,
Was featured in Domum Improvius.

An Old Man of Vesuvius

A Man of Dundee

There was an Old Man of Dundee,
Who frequented the top of a tree;
When disturbed by the Crows, he abruptly arose,
And exclaimed, "I'll return to Dundee!"

Edward Lear

There was an Old Man of Dundee,
With a home in the branches, so twee;
When a crow that could talk
Cackled "Pass me a fork!"
He just laughed himself out of the tree.

A Lady Whose Folly

There was an Old Lady whose folly
Induced her to sit in a holly;
Whereon, by a thorn her dress being torn,
She quickly became melancholy.

Edward Lear

There was an Old Lady whose folly
Was built at the base of a holly;
And when feeling aloof
She would climb on the roof,
And just sit in the tree with her collie.

A Man On Some Rocks

There was an Old Man on some rocks,
Who shut his Wife up in a box:
When she said, "Let me out," he exclaimed,
"Without doubt
You will pass all your life in that box."

Edward Lear

There was an Old Man of the Rocks,
Who locked an old bag in a box;
"Never leave me alone!"
She implored, with a groan,
So he added his smelly old socks.

A Person of Rheims

There was an Old Person of Rheims,
Who was troubled with horrible dreams;
So to keep him awake they fed him with cake,
Which amused that Old Person of Rheims.

Edward Lear

There was an Old Person of Rheims,
Who was troubled with terrible dreams,
Of his pantry beset
By intruders, unmet,
And they took all his Coffee and Creams.

A Man of Leghorn

There was an Old Man of Leghorn,
The smallest that ever was born;
But quickly snapt up he was once by a Puppy,
Who devoured that Old Man of Leghorn.

Edward Lear

There was an Old Man of Leghorn,
The smallest who ever was born;
He would ride on his pup,
Which could fit in a cup,
And the walkers he treated with scorn.

A Man In a Pew

There was an Old Man in a pew,
Whose waistcoat was spotted with blue;
But he tore it in pieces, to give to his Nieces,
That cheerful Old Man in a pew.

Edward Lear

There was an Old Man in a pew,
Whose waistcoat was ripped the way through,
And his collar was twisted ...
The priest had insisted
Communion be done in a queue.

A Man of Jamaica

There was an Old Man of Jamaica,
Who suddenly married a Quaker;
But she cried out, "Oh, lack! I have married a
black!"
Which distressed that Old Man of Jamaica.

Edward Lear

A beach-combing Man of Jamaica
Found a shipwrecked and castaway Quaker;
So they walked up the sand
With a hand in a hand,
And got muffins and rolls from the baker.

A Man Who Said How

*There was an Old Man who said, "How
Shall I flee from this horrible Cow?
I will sit on this stile, and continue to smile,
Which may soften the heart of that Cow."*

Edward Lear

*"Get me free of this cow!" said the man
On a rural retreat from Milan;
But the cow, for her part,
Who was studying art,
Took her pencil and captured the man.*

A Lady of Troy

There was a Young Lady of Troy,
Whom several large flies did annoy;
Some she killed with a thump, some she
drowned at the pump,
And some she took with her to Troy.

Edward Lear

There was a Young Lady of Troy,
Who was bothered by flies, and a boy;
She could flick at the flies,
But in spite of her sighs,
How the boy did enjoy to annoy!

A Lady of Hull

There was a Young Lady of Hull,
Who was chased by a virulent Bull;
But she seized on a spade, and called out,
"Who's afraid?"
Which distracted that virulent Bull.

Edward Lear

*There was a Young Lady of **Hull**,*
*Who was chased by a virulent **Bull**;*
And she fell in a heap,
With a little black sheep ...
*She was lucky his bags were all **full**.*

A Young Lady of Hull

A Person of Dutton

There was an Old Person of Dutton,
Whose head was as small as a button;
So to make it look big he purchased a wig,
And rapidly rushed about Dutton.

Edward Lear

A small-headed chap of Van Nuys
Ate to bolster his cranial size;
But he bit on a button
In mutton from Dutton,
And swallowed a tooth in surprise.

A Man Who Said Hush

There was an Old Man who said, "Hush!
I perceive a young bird in this bush!"
When they said, "Is it small?" he replied, "Not at all;
It is four times as big as the bush!"

Edward Lear

*There was an Old Man who said, "**Hush!***
*It's a Totalitarian **Thrush!**"*
Then it had him arrested,
And tortured and tested,
*And sent to a camp in the **bush**.*

A Lady of Russia

There was a Young Lady of Russia,
Who screamed so that no one could hush her;
Her screams were extreme,—no one heard
such a scream
As was screamed by that Lady of Russia.

Edward Lear

A Pallid-Faced Lady of Russia
Liked to redden her cheeks with a blusher;
And she travelled to Bruges
To acquire more rouge,
Though the blusher in Russia was plusher.

A Lady of Tyre

There was a Young Lady of Tyre,
Who swept the loud chords of a lyre;
At the sound of each sweep she enraptured the deep,
And enchanted the city of Tyre.

Edward Lear

There was a Young Lady of Tyre
Who set an old woman on fire,
Whom she'd earlier fled,
So as not to be dead,
And to Smyrna she now could retire.

A Person of Bangor

There was an Old Person of Bangor,
Whose face was distorted with anger;
He tore off his boots, and subsisted on roots,
That borascible Person of Bangor.

Edward Lear

He opened the door and, agleam,
Took the box that enfolded his dream;
Then contorted with anger
Cause someone in Bangor
Put anchovies on his Supreme.

A Man of the East

There was an Old Man of the East,
Who gave all his children a feast;
But they all ate so much, and their conduct was such,
That it killed that Old Man of the East.

Edward Lear

A man of the East, with a frown,
Rode his powerful beast through the town;
Back and forth, to and fro,
For a decade or so,
Cause he didn't know how to get down.

A Man of the Coast

There was an Old Man of the Coast,
Who placidly sat on a post;
But when it was cold he relinquished his hold,
And called for some hot buttered toast.

Edward Lear

There was an Old Man of the Coast,
Who sat all day long on a post;
Though you'd think, for a cert,
That his bottom would hurt,
In the end, he was tougher than most.

A Man of Kamschatka

There was an Old Man of Kamschatka,
Who possessed a remarkably fat Cur;
His gait and his waddle were held as a model
To all the fat dogs in Kamschatka.

Edward Lear

There was an Old Man of Kamschatka,
Whose daughter arrived for a chatka;
The Man was delighted,
The Dog was excited ...
The Cat only sat on the matka.

A Person of Gretna

There was an Old Person of Gretna,
Who rushed down the crater of Etna;
When they said, "Is it hot?" he replied, "No, it's not!"
That mendacious Old Person of Gretna.

Edward Lear

There was an Old Man with his ret'na
Full trained on the fires of Etna;
And he said "What a spot!
But it's overly hot,
And the grass is much greener in Gretna."

A Man With a Beard

There was an Old Man with a beard,
Who sat on a Horse when he reared;
But they said, "Never mind! you will fall off
behind,
You propitious Old Man with a beard!"

Edward Lear

There was an Old Man of the Weird,
Who whinnied and suddenly reared;
For he'd hidden, perforce,
In his whiskers, a horse,
And it now ran away with his beard.

A Man of Berlin

There was an Old Man of Berlin,
Whose form was uncommonly thin;
Till he once, by mistake, was mixed up in a cake,
So they baked that Old Man of Berlin.

Edward Lear

There was an Old Man of Berlin,
Whose form was uncommonly thin;
So he'd drop to the floor
And go under the door
When his wife wouldn't let him come in.

A Man of the West

*There was an Old Man of the West,
Who never could get any rest;
So they set him to spin on his nose and his chin,
Which cured that Old Man of the West.*

Edward Lear

*There was an Old Man of the West,
Who slept in a bullet-proof vest,
Out of fear of invasion;
But constant abrasion
Would often inhibit his rest.*

A Person of Cheadle

There was an Old Person of Cheadle
Was put in the stocks by the Beadle
For stealing some pigs, some coats, and some wigs,
That horrible person of Cheadle.

Edward Lear

There was an Old Person of Cheadle
Who drove through the village at speedle;
He was put in the stocks
With a great many locks,
For the Beadle was deaf to his wheedle.

A Person of Anerley

There was an Old Person of Anerley,
Whose conduct was strange and unmannerly;
He rushed down the Strand with a Pig in each hand,
But returned in the evening to Anerley.

Edward Lear

There was an Old Spectre of Anerley,
Who wandered the city uncannily;
But his belching and farting,
Forever restarting,
Were not very ghost-like, or mannerly.

A Lady of Wales

There was a Young Lady of Wales,
Who caught a large Fish without scales;
When she lifted her hook, she exclaimed,
"Only look!"
That ecstatic Young Lady of Wales.

Edward Lear

There was a Young Lady of Wales
Who balanced her weight on the scales,
With a dog and a fox,
And a little pink box
That contained her collection of snails.

A Lady of Welling

*There was a Young Lady of Welling,
Whose praise all the world was a-telling;
She played on the harp, and caught several Carp,
That accomplished Young Lady of Welling.*

Edward Lear

*There was a Young Lady of Welling,
Whose brother was constantly yelling,
Which she couldn't abide,
So she took him inside,
And insisted he finish his spelling.*

A Person of Tartary

There was an Old Person of Tartary,
Who divided his jugular artery;
But he screeched to his Wife, and she said,
"Oh, my life!
Your death will be felt by all Tartary!"

Edward Lear

There was an Old Person of Tartary,
Who stopped at a little-known martyry,
With the top of the head
Of the rapturous dead,
And a piece of the jugular artery.

A Man of Whitehaven

*There was an Old Man of Whitehaven,
Who danced a quadrille with a Raven;
But they said, "It's absurd to encourage this bird!"
So they smashed that Old Man of Whitehaven.*

Edward Lear

*There was an Old Person of Mudgee
Who danced a quadrille with a Budgie;
But they left, with regret,
At the end of the set,
Because everyone there was so judgy.*

A Lady of Sweden

There was a Young Lady of Sweden,
Who went by the slow train to Weedon;
When they cried, "Weedon Station!" she made
no observation,
But thought she should go back to Sweden.

  Edward Lear

A Lady who'd travelled from Sweden,
And wanted to visit each Weedon,
Went to Weedon and Weedon
And Weedon Bec (Weedon),
And finished her journey in Wieden.

A Person of Chester

There was an Old Person of Chester,
Whom several small children did pester;
They threw some large stones, which broke
most of his bones,
And displeased that Old Person of Chester.

Edward Lear

There was a Young Lady of Chester
Who found a Young Fellow to pester;
Though he'd constantly say
That he wished her away,
His insouciance really impressed her.

A Man of the Cape

*There was an Old Man of the Cape,
Who possessed a large Barbary Ape;
Till the Ape, one dark night, set the house all alight,
Which burned that Old Man of the Cape.*

Edward Lear

*There was an Old Man of the Cape,
Who lived with a Barbary Ape,
In a crumbling house,
With a musical mouse,
And a spider that couldn't escape.*

An Old Man of the Cape

A Person of Burton

There was an Old Person of Burton,
Whose answers were rather uncertain;
When they said, "How d'ye do?" he replied,
"Who are you?"
That distressing Old Person of Burton.

Edward Lear

There was an Old Person of Burton,
Who hid every day in the curtain;
When they asked what he feared,
He at last volunteered
That he honestly couldn't be certain.

A Person of Ems

There was an Old Person of Ems
Who casually fell in the Thames;
And when he was found, they said he was drowned,
That unlucky Old Person of Ems.

Edward Lear

There was an Old Person of Ems,
A village immersed in the Thames,
Who could breathe with a reed,
Though he hadn't the need,
For his air was all there in the Thames.

A Girl of Majorca

There was a Young Girl of Majorca,
Whose Aunt was a very fast walker;
She walked seventy miles, and leaped fifteen
stiles,
Which astonished that Girl of Majorca.

Edward Lear

There was a Young Girl of Majorca,
Who rode on the back of an orca,
And she called to her aunt
To go slower. "I can't!"
Cause her aunt was a very fast walker.

A Lady of Poole

There was a Young Lady of Poole,
Whose soup was excessively cool;
So she put it to boil by the aid of some oil,
That ingenious Young Lady of Poole.

Edward Lear

There was a Young Lady of Poole,
Who sat by the side of the pool,
With a gigglesome bunch
For an hour past lunch,
Cause her mother had said it's a rule.

A Lady of Prague

There was an Old Lady of Prague,
Whose language was horribly vague;
When they said, "Are these caps?" she
answered, "Perhaps!"
That oracular Lady of Prague.

Edward Lear

There was a young lady of Prague-o
Who flaunted the travel embargo;
Yet it wasn't a crime,
As she travelled in Time,
And awoke on the deck of the Argo.

A Lady of Parma

There was a Young Lady of Parma,
Whose conduct grew calmer and calmer:
When they said, "Are you dumb?" she merely
said, "Hum!"
That provoking Young Lady of Parma.

Edward Lear

There was a Young Lady of Parma,
Who swam with a panicking llama;
But her friend from Majorca
Appeared on her orca,
And Palmer (the llama) was calmer.

A Person of Sparta

There was an Old Person of Sparta,
Who had twenty-five sons and one "darter;"
He fed them on Snails, and weighed them in scales,
That wonderful Person of Sparta.

Edward Lear

There was a Young Person of Sparta,
Who carried a note in her garter:
"Should the bearer be found
Unattended, but sound,
This address is the home of her mater."

A Man On Whose Nose

There was an Old Man on whose nose
Most birds of the air could repose;
But they all flew away at the closing of day,
Which relieved that Old Man and his nose.

Edward Lear

There was an Old Man who would pose
With a scarecrow of ribbons and bows,
In his grim understanding
That birds would be landing
To sit on his prominent nose.

A Lady of Turkey

There was a Young Lady of Turkey,
Who wept when the weather was murky;
When the day turned out fine, she ceased to repine,
That capricious Young Lady of Turkey.

Edward Lear

There was a Young Lady of Turkey,
Who liked to be chewing on jerky;
Just the tiniest quibble,
She tended to dribble,
And oh! Her saliva was irky!

A Man of Aosta

There was an Old Man of Aosta
Who possessed a large Cow, but he lost her;
But they said, "Don't you see she has run up a tree,
You invidious Old Man of Aosta?"

Edward Lear

There was an Old Man of Aosta
Who had an old cow but he lost her,
Having slyly departed,
The moment she started
To walk to the counter at Costa.

A Person of Crete

There was a Young Person of Crete,
Whose toilette was far from complete;
She dressed in a sack spickle-speckled with black,
That ombliferous Person of Crete.

Edward Lear

There was a Young Person of Crete,
Whose toilette was far from complete;
But she vaulted a bull
And she floated like wool,
Having always been light on her feet.

A Young Person of Crete

A Lady of Clare

There was a Young Lady of Clare,
Who was madly pursued by a Bear;
When she found she was tired, she abruptly expired,
That unfortunate Lady of Clare.

Edward Lear

There was a Young Lady of Clare,
Who found herself sued by a Bear,
Who alleged she had lifted
A coat he'd been gifted,
And thereby had rendered him bare.

A Lady of Dorking

There was a Young Lady of Dorking,
Who bought a large bonnet for walking;
But its colour and size so bedazzled her eyes,
That she very soon went back to Dorking.

Edward Lear

There was a Young Lady of Dorking,
Who'd leave when her mouth began talking;
But bearing in mind
Correspondents behind,
She would never look where she was walking.

A Man of Cape Horn

There was an Old Man of Cape Horn,
Who wished he had never been born;
So he sat on a Chair till he died of despair,
That dolorous Man of Cape Horn.

Edward Lear

There was an Old Man of Cape Horn,
Who fell in the Doldrums one morn;
He was saved by a horse
That could swim, so of course,
He made sure it had plenty of corn.

A Person of Cromer

There was an old Person of Cromer,
Who stood on one leg to read Homer;
When he found he grew stiff, he jumped over
the cliff,
Which concluded that Person of Cromer.

Edward Lear

There was an Old Person of Cromer
Who stood on one leg to read Homer;
On the other he'd read
From the Venerable Bede,
But Biggles he kept for Tacoma.

A Man of the Hague

There was an Old Man of the Hague,
Whose ideas were excessively vague;
He built a balloon to examine the moon,
That deluded Old Man of the Hague.

Edward Lear

There was a Young Man of Den Haag
Who travelled the world with a duck,
A wonderful quacker
That worked as a hacker
By night, and by day was a duck.

A Person of Spain

There was an Old Person of Spain,
Who hated all trouble and pain;
So he sate on a chair with his feet in the air,
That umbrageous Old Person of Spain.

Edward Lear

The Airports, a feature of Spain,
Had of course to be built on the plain,
Where the weather, they boast,
Will precipitate most,
So in Spain you emplane in the rain.

A Man Who Said Well

There was an Old Man who said, "Well!
Will nobody answer this bell?
I have pulled day and night, till my hair has
grown white,
But nobody answers this bell!"

  Edward Lear

There was an Old Man who'd done well,
Only no one would answer his bell;
So he fired a shot
At the ceiling and got
A response: he must leave the hotel.

A Man With an Owl

There was an Old Man with an Owl,
Who continued to bother and howl;
He sat on a rail, and imbibed bitter ale,
Which refreshed that Old Man and his Owl.

Edward Lear

There was an Old Man with an owl
Which he covered each day with a towel;
But the owl took flight
With the towel at night
As an owl on the prowl in a cowl.

A Man in a Casement

There was an Old Man in a casement,
Who held up his hands in amazement;
When they said, "Sir, you'll fall!" he replied,
"Not at all!"
That incipient Old Man in a casement.

Edward Lear

There was an Old Man in a casement,
And nothing could shake his emplacement;
Looking down with disdain,
He declared he'd remain
Until somebody found a replacement.

A Person of Ewell

There was an Old Person of Ewell,
Who chiefly subsisted on gruel;
But to make it more nice, he inserted some
Mice,
Which refreshed that Old Person of Ewell.

Edward Lear

There was an Old Person of Ewell,
Who travelled to Ultima Thule;
When his journey was done
He was where he'd begun,
Which was good, cause he'd run out of fuel.

A Man of Peru

There was an Old Man of Peru.
Who never knew what he should do;
So he tore off his hair, and behaved like a bear,
That intrinsic Old Man of Peru.

Edward Lear

There was an Old Man of Peru,
Who sat on a tuffet, all blue;
But an Eider had spied him,
And sat down beside him,
And gave him a sip of its brew.

A Man With a Beard

There was an Old Man with a beard,
Who said, "It is just as I feared!—
Two Owls and a Hen, four Larks and a Wren,
Have all built their nests in my beard."

Edward Lear

There was an old man who was cheered,
When the birds made a home in his beard;
But the ostrich was banned,
On account of the sand,
So it stood at the window and sneered.

A Man Who Was Cheered

A Lady Whose Eyes

There was a Young Lady whose eyes
Were unique as to colour and size;
When she opened them wide, people all turned aside,
And started away in surprise.

Edward Lear

There was a Young Lady whose eyes
Were of different colours (same size);
So she'd cry in her bed
Till her eyes were both red,
Whereupon would she happily rise.

A Lady of Ryde

*There was a Young Lady of Ryde,
Whose shoe-strings were seldom untied;
She purchased some clogs, and some small spotty Dogs,
And frequently walked about Ryde.*

Edward Lear

*There was a Young Lady of Ryde,
Who took life's events in her stride;
But in spite of all that
She would often fall flat,
For her shoes were forever untied.*

A Lady Whose Bonnet

There was a Young Lady whose bonnet
Came untied when the birds sate upon it;
But she said, "I don't care! all the birds in the air
Are welcome to sit on my bonnet!"

Edward Lear

There was a Young Lady whose bonnet
Aroused envy whenever she'd don it;
She was ever so proud
Of its look in a crowd,
But was crushed when a bottom sat on it.

The Next Hundred Lears

Limericks After Lear Book Two

In 1872, Edward Lear published one hundred new limericks. But while his verses from *A Book of Nonsense* are still fondly remembered today, still anthologised, still quoted in mainstream and social media, his next hundred limericks, his last, are unknown.

Why?

Because the limerick had its own life by 1872, and was romping towards the twentieth century with outlandish, irreverent and often obscene delight. Lear couldn't - or perhaps he wouldn't - provide the style of limerick that readers were demanding, let alone its content.

So having set the little verse on its journey, the Father of the Limerick now stood alone and watched it vanish in the distance.

The Next Hundred Lears, Book Two in this series, unearths the lost one hundred limericks of Edward Lear and presents them complete. Each original is paired with a brand new version that deploys with all the shameless, giggle-hunting intent of a true limerick.

But family-friendly :)

"*The Next Hundred Lears* is a book to make you smile."

Sascha Martin's Rocket-Ship

"Misadventures have never been so much fun"

Reviews

5.0 out of 5 stars A joy to read!

"My sons and I absolutely LOVED this take on a science experiment gone wrong. It had a lot of humour, the rhyme was complex but worked well, and the illustrations were spot on! Misadventures have never been so much fun…"

Amazon Reviewer

5.0 out of 5 stars Really enjoyed the rhyming story.

"Hilarious, entertaining story, creative thinking, fun to read over and over again, imaginative, loved, loved, loved it, colorful pictures, wonderful science fiction"

Amazon Reviewer

5.0 out of 5 stars Great read!

"Short and sweet! Excellent book to read with my daughter and we loved all of the perfect rhyming and humor!"

Amazon Reviewer

5.0 out of 5 stars Very Entertaining!

"I found this book to be absolutely delightful! I read the book to myself and got a great chuckle out of the story."

Amazon Reviewer

5.0 out of 5 stars Great read

"Daughter loved it found it hilarious

"And cool she says"

Amazon Reviewer

5.0 out of 5 stars What a trip!

"A fun book to read. Certainly not a bedtime story, so full of action. My grandsons loved it."

Amazon Reviewer

5.0 out of 5 stars Super cute!

"I am 46 with no kids but I love children's books. This book was excellent! Very funny and wonderful artwork! I highly recommend for any age!"

Amazon Reviewer

5.0 out of 5 stars Hilariously

"Sascha Martin is so very very very funny…

"That's why I love this book so so much."

Amazon Reviewer

Thank You

Thanks for reading The Next Hundred Lears. I do hope you enjoyed the limericks, or some of them at least. If you're up for writing a review, that would be just ... amazing!!! ... because reviews help books (and me!) find new readers.

Discover More

Read more limericks, read about limericks, sign up for a newsletter, look in on the *Sascha Martin* books, or just reach out and say hi, all at ...

KidsBooke.com

www.ingramcontent.com/pod-product-compliance
Lightning Source LLC
Chambersburg PA
CBHW050316010526
44107CB00055B/2269